Explorations

DARWIN IN THE GALÁPAGOS

BY DALTON RAINS

WWW.APEXEDITIONS.COM

Copyright © 2025 by Apex Editions, Mendota Heights, MN 55120. All rights reserved. No part of this book may be reproduced or utilized in any form or by any means without written permission from the publisher.

Apex is distributed by North Star Editions:
sales@northstareditions.com | 888-417-0195

Produced for Apex by Red Line Editorial.

Photographs ©: Universal Images Group/Getty Images, cover; Shutterstock Images, 1, 8, 10–11, 13, 14–15, 18, 19, 20, 25; Chroma Collection/Alamy, 4–5, 22–23; Artepics/Alamy, 7; iStockphoto, 9, 26–27, 29; NASA, 16–17; Foto-zone/Alamy, 21; The Print Collector/Hulton Fine Art Collection/Getty Images, 24

Library of Congress Control Number: 2024940541

ISBN
979-8-89250-327-3 (hardcover)
979-8-89250-365-5 (paperback)
979-8-89250-438-6 (ebook pdf)
979-8-89250-403-4 (hosted ebook)

Printed in the United States of America
Mankato, MN
012025

NOTE TO PARENTS AND EDUCATORS

Apex books are designed to build literacy skills in striving readers. Exciting, high-interest content attracts and holds readers' attention. The text is carefully leveled to allow students to achieve success quickly. Additional features, such as bolded glossary words for difficult terms, help build comprehension.

CHAPTER 1
SETTING SAIL 4

CHAPTER 2
EXPLORING CHILE 10

CHAPTER 3
THE GALÁPAGOS 16

CHAPTER 4
NEW IDEAS 22

COMPREHENSION QUESTIONS • 28
GLOSSARY • 30
TO LEARN MORE • 31
ABOUT THE AUTHOR • 31
INDEX • 32

CHAPTER 1

SETTING SAIL

On December 27, 1831, the HMS *Beagle* set sail. Its crew planned to make maps of South America. A **naturalist** traveled with them. His name was Charles Darwin.

The HMS *Beagle* started in England. It sailed around the world.

The *Beagle* stopped at some islands. Then, it sailed down South America's coast. Darwin made several trips inland. He studied rocks and animals. He also dug up **fossils**.

FAST FACT
Darwin often stayed on land for days or weeks at a time.

Charles Darwin was 22 years old when the *Beagle*'s journey began.

The ship reached Argentina by September 1832. There, Darwin found fossils of huge **mammals**. He wondered why the animals had died.

Darwin found several types of fossils. Some were from ground sloths.

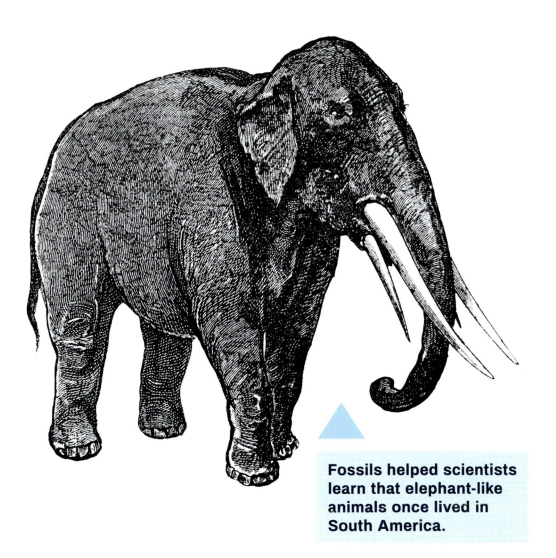

Fossils helped scientists learn that elephant-like animals once lived in South America.

BIG BONES

Later, scientists studied the fossils Darwin found. They tried to learn what animals the bones came from. They identified several new types of **extinct** animals.

CHAPTER 2

EXPLORING CHILE

Next, the *Beagle* sailed to Chile. Darwin saw a volcano erupt there in January 1835. The next month, he felt an **earthquake**. It destroyed a nearby town.

Osorno Volcano is in southern Chile. It erupted 11 times between 1575 and 1869.

Near the town, Darwin saw mussel beds. Mussels need water. But these beds were above high tide. The earthquake had moved the land.

SHIFTING LAND

Back in 1832, Darwin had found oyster shells in rock. The rock was high in the mountains. But Darwin thought a sea once covered the area. The land moved higher over time.

Mussels attach to rocks. To stay alive, they must be covered in water at least part of the time.

The Andes Mountains run through several countries in South America. Darwin thought a series of earthquakes created them.

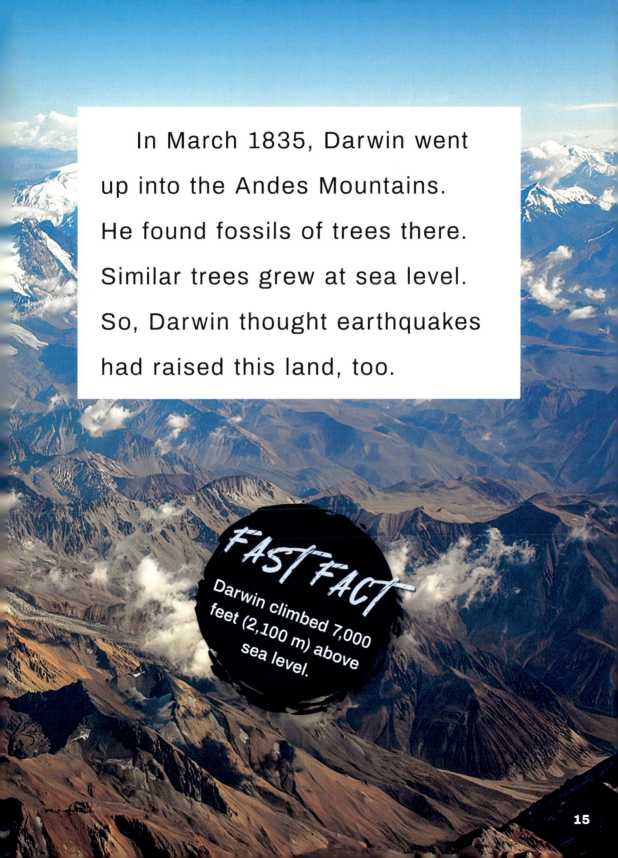

In March 1835, Darwin went up into the Andes Mountains. He found fossils of trees there. Similar trees grew at sea level. So, Darwin thought earthquakes had raised this land, too.

FAST FACT
Darwin climbed 7,000 feet (2,100 m) above sea level.

CHAPTER 3

THE GALÁPAGOS

From Chile, the *Beagle* traveled north and west. It arrived at the Galápagos Islands in September 1835.

The Galápagos Islands are about 600 miles (1,000 km) west of South America.

Some birds on the Galápagos Islands had wider beaks than others.

Darwin visited four islands. He studied their plants and animals. Darwin noticed several types of small birds. On each island, their beaks looked a bit different. Their color varied, too.

FAST FACT
Darwin found a tortoise on one island. He kept it as a pet.

Several types of giant tortoises live on the Galápagos Islands.

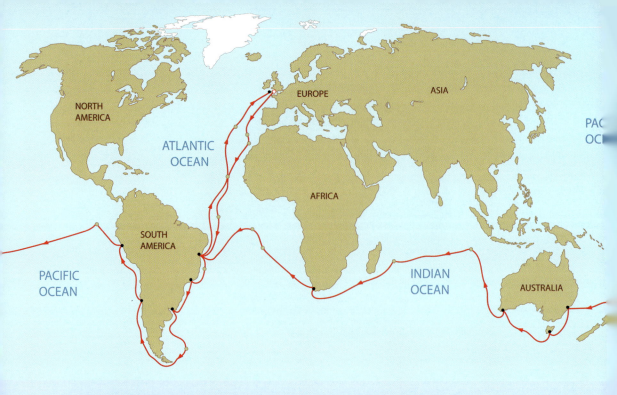

The *Beagle* sailed past both Australia and Africa.

Darwin and the ship's crew collected birds from several islands. Then, the *Beagle* continued west. It visited islands in the Pacific Ocean.

TAKING NOTES

Darwin kept a diary during the *Beagle*'s voyage. He also wrote 1,750 pages of notes. They described what he collected and learned. Darwin also drew pictures of his **specimens**.

Darwin's diary was 770 pages long.

CHAPTER 4

NEW IDEAS

Darwin arrived home in October 1836. He published his notes. He also sent specimens to experts around England. They helped study the plants and animals he found.

On the way home, the *Beagle* stopped in South America to remap part of the coast.

1. Geospiza magnirostris.
3. Geospiza parvula.
2. Geospiza fortis.
4. Certhidea olivasea.

About 15 different types of finches live on the Galápagos Islands.

One scientist identified the birds from the Galápagos Islands. He found many types of finches. All shared an ancestor. One finch **species** had come to the islands from South America.

NEW SPECIES

Finches on different islands ate different foods. Some ate insects. Others ate seeds. Different beak shapes helped the birds eat these foods. Over time, new species formed.

Birds that ate cactuses had longer, more-pointed beaks.

Darwin continued thinking about how big changes can happen over time. He formed the theory of **evolution** by **natural selection**. This idea changed science forever.

FAST FACT

In 1859, Darwin published his ideas in a book called *On the Origin of Species*.

Darwin waited many years before publishing his ideas about natural selection.

COMPREHENSION QUESTIONS

Write your answers on a separate piece of paper.

1. Write a few sentences describing the main ideas of Chapter 2.

2. Would you rather study living animals or fossils from long ago? Why?

3. In what year did the HMS *Beagle* begin its voyage?
    - A. 1831
    - B. 1835
    - C. 1836

4. In what year did Darwin experience an earthquake?
    - A. 1831
    - B. 1835
    - C. 1836

5. What does **varied** mean in this book?

*On each island, their beaks looked a bit different. Their color **varied**, too.*

    A. was exactly alike
    B. was a bit different
    C. was all black

6. What does **ancestor** mean in this book?

*He found many types of finches. All shared an **ancestor**. One finch species had come to the islands from South America.*

    A. an animal that other animals eat
    B. an animal that other animals mate with
    C. an animal that other animals are related to

Answer key on page 32.

GLOSSARY

earthquake
An event where part of Earth shakes or trembles.

evolution
The process of animals changing slowly over time.

extinct
No longer living on Earth.

fossils
Remains of plants and animals that lived long ago.

mammals
Animals that have hair and produce milk for their young.

naturalist
A person who studies nature, often by exploring outside.

natural selection
When living things with helpful traits pass those traits on.

species
A group of animals or plants that are similar and can breed with one another.

specimens
Examples of plants or animals that are collected and studied.

BOOKS

Hansen, Grace. *Dinosaur Graveyards in South America.* Minneapolis: Abdo Publishing, 2022.

Rathburn, Betsy. *Exploring the Amazon.* Minneapolis: Bellwether Media, 2023.

Sipperley, Keli. *Fossils.* North Mankato, MN: Capstone Press, 2021.

ONLINE RESOURCES

Visit **www.apexeditions.com** to find links and resources related to this title.

ABOUT THE AUTHOR

Dalton Rains is an author and editor from Saint Paul, Minnesota.

INDEX

A
Andes Mountains, 15
Argentina, 8

C
Chile, 10, 16

E
earthquakes, 10, 12, 15
evolution, 26

F
finches, 24–25
fossils, 6, 8–9, 15

G
Galápagos Islands, 16, 24

H
HMS *Beagle*, 4, 6, 10, 16, 20–21

M
mussels, 12

N
natural selection, 26
notes, 21, 22

O
On the Origin of Species, 26

P
Pacific Ocean, 20

S
South America, 4, 6, 24
specimens, 21, 22

ANSWER KEY:
1. Answers will vary; 2. Answers will vary; 3. A; 4. B; 5. B; 6. C